To the version of you who knows you can …
let's go prove her right!

"I work with artists and I'm going to recommend this book to all of them. This is what we need to know about things like pricing, imposter syndrome, and the ubiquitous social media. And her advice is practical, manageable, sustainable and proven."

FRAN GARDNER, artist, writer, consultant, and author of the Artists Will Find a Way series

"Shana's book is a must read for new online business owners. Honestly, it is a great read for seasoned business owners as well. I read this with a beginner's mindset and gained new and valuable insights. The way this book is written is easily digestible. It provides step-by-step guidance, real talk, questions for gaining clarity and is extremely empowering. "

JANA SALVATORE, Author, Founder of Off Kilter Co., ICF Certified Transformational, Embodiment, and Human Design Coach

"This book is for those who are tired of being boxed in and want to know how to make their "zone of genius" be the thing that pays the bills. Shana's honesty blended with practicality is just what those of us who want to bust out of the box need."

CINDY URBANKSI, author of *Evolving from the Roots: The Magic in the Work*

SH*T
NO ONE
TELLS YOU

About Starting an
Online Business

SHANA V. HARTMAN, PHD

SYNERGY
PUBLISHING GROUP

BELMONT, NORTH CAROLINA

Sh*t No One Tells You About Starting an Online Business
Shana V. Hartman, PhD

Published by Synergy Publishing Group, Belmont, NC
Layout and design by Melisa Graham

Softcover, January 2026, ISBN 978-1-960892-62-1
Ebook, January 2026, ISBN 978-1-960892-63-8

Contents

What the Hell Are You Thinking by Starting a Business?

AND WHY I MAY KNOW THE ANSWER!

From salaried English professor to $49 Massages to $50K Programs (and Why This Book Exists)

I thought I was going to be a university English professor forever. From the moment I stepped onto the campus of East Carolina University as a freshman in 1996, I was hooked. The schedule, the freedom, the trees, the ability to wander around thinking deep thoughts and asking big questions—I thought, *Yes. This is it. This is where I want to be for the rest of my life.*

It's not surprising, really. I value freedom highly. I don't like being told what to do and how to be (understatement). But by 2014, the magic had worn off. I was a tenured professor with nowhere left to grow. The only motivation left was internal, and even that was hard to muster in an environment that didn't support innovation or change.

I started looking for a way out.

I thought I could pivot to corporate work—training employees, designing curriculum—but despite my skill set and education, the doors didn't open. I applied for job after job and got radio silence. I needed something of my own. A space to explore. Something that could make me a little extra money and bring me back to myself.

So I got licensed as a massage therapist. Yes, really. In 2017, I opened a tiny side hustle in the basement of my house while still teaching full time, raising three kids, and checking all the boxes of what my life *should* look like. That little practice grew over the next two years. By 2019, I had founded **Synergy Wellness Group LLC**, opened a brick-and-mortar space, and started coaching—both in person and online—women who were doing all the things and slowly losing themselves in the process. (Hi, it was me. I was the woman in that sentence.)

I knew massage would not be my "way out," so I leaned more into coaching. That same year, I started investing in myself in strategic ways. I was coaching, learning, getting certified in the BodyMind Method(™), and discovering what was possible when I took myself—and this business—seriously.

Then the pandemic hit.

And I realized: holy sh*t, I can work with people *virtually*. From anywhere. While I had taught virtually and asynchronously as a professor, I realized there was even more potential with my coaching business. I started experimenting with different coaching, different offers, and different pricing models. And in 2020, I landed my first $10K client. I knew right then that this wasn't just a cute side hustle anymore. This was my path out of academia.

By May 2021, I had taught my last college class and fully stepped into coaching and business ownership. I merged my love of writing and expression with the coaching tools I had developed, and **Synergy Publishing Group** was born.

Now? That coaching, writing support, and publishing are at the heart of my business. And everything I've learned from the rollercoaster ride of academia to massage therapy to multiple five-figure coaching offers has shaped who I am and how I support others. Since then, I've also partnered in the evolution of Synergy Wellness Group and co-founded **Synergy House LLC**, a lakefront retreat space for short-term rentals, small gatherings, and transformational events on Lake Norman in Troutman, North Carolina.

I know this all might sound like bat-shit craziness. I get it. How did I go from $49 massages to $50K programs?

That's exactly what I want to unpack in this book. Spoiler alert: it has been an amazingly messy journey!

I'm sharing what I've learned from trial and error, incredible mentors, generous colleagues, brilliant clients, and my own inner knowing. Not because I have all the answers (hint: I don't), but because I know how overwhelming and confusing the online business space can be. Everything looks either wildly scammy or like a full-time hustle with no joy in sight.

This book is for you if:

- ★ You've felt the nudge to build a business—*your* business
- ★ You want to do it in a way that actually honors your energy, your values, your boundaries, and your vision.
- ★ You desire a business that supports your *life*, not the other way around.

I'm not the top expert. But I know this: most of the business books out there are still pretty male, pale, and stale. I wanted to offer something else— something real, a bit fiery, deeply human, and rooted in the belief that good people can do incredible things in the world *and* get paid well for it.

If that sounds like your vibe, then you're in the right place. I'm so glad you're here. Let's get started.

What to Expect in This Book

This isn't your typical business book.

You won't find rigid formulas, 10-step blueprints, or any talk about "crushing it." What you *will* find is real talk, personal stories, practical tools, and a lot of truth-telling about what it actually takes to start and grow a heart-centered online business—without losing your soul (or your mind).

Each chapter blends:

* ★ **Mindset shifts** you *actually* need to make this sustainable
* ★ **Business insights** drawn from real-life experience (mine and others')
* ★ **Gut checks** to help you take aligned action
* ★ **Reminders to trust yourself** because your business should work *for you*

You'll also find two bonus worksheets at key points in the book:

* A **Visibility Gut Check Worksheet** to help you get started even if you're unsure where to begin
* A **Boundary-Setting Worksheet** so you can protect your time, energy, and vision

Most chapters can standalone, so bounce around if that's your style. And if you find yourself laughing, nodding, or side-eyeing your comfort zone—that's on purpose.

I wrote this book to honor the brave beginning, the messy middle, and the rebellious heart who wants to keep going, knowing there's got to be a better way to do this whole "business" thing. Let's dive in!

The confidence won't arrive before you begin—it'll meet you on the road.

CHAPTER 1

What Business Should I Start?

HINT: THERE'S NO PERFECT IDEA

The Most Googled Question That Will Never Give You the Answer

If you've found yourself deep in a rabbit hole of:

> "Profitable online business ideas"
> "Side hustles I can start with no money"
> "How to know which business idea is *the one*"

Then, hi, and welcome to the club where overthinkers, perfectionists, and wildly capable humans have been tricked into thinking there's a "right" answer waiting on page six of a Pinterest board.

Spoiler: There isn't. And the longer you *wait* for clarity, for the *one* right answer, the longer you delay momentum and actually do what you came here to do: start an online business.

Why You're Probably Stuck

If you're stuck on what business to start, you're likely not short on ideas—you're drowning in **self-doubt.**

Let's name what's *really* going on:

- ★ "But what if I pick the wrong thing?"
- ★ "I have too many passions; I can't choose!"
- ★ "What if no one wants this?"
- ★ "I'm not an expert, so who am I to teach/sell/create?"
- ★ "Someone else is already doing it (and doing it better)."

Analysis paralysis isn't about a lack of information. It's about fear of doing it wrong and being seen trying.

The Myth of "The One Perfect Idea"

Here's the truth no one tells you: There are **many** ideas you could run with. And every successful entrepreneur you admire? They probably started with something *totally different* from what they're known for now.

For Example:

★ That multi-six-figure coach? Started with a blog no one read.
★ That thriving online shop owner? Their first product flopped.
★ That course creator with the fancy sales funnel?[1] Had four failed launches[2] before the fifth hit.

The key isn't in finding *the* idea.
It's choosing *an* idea—and letting it evolve.

---

1. "Sales Funnel" can seem like a fancy business term, but I think of it as the journey a potential client goes on from initially "meeting/ finding" me (aka a cold lead) to becoming a paying client. You will have plenty of people that follow you online, are on your email list, etc., but the process of filtering that larger audience to paying clients is the "funnel."
2. "Launch" is a term used for when your offer, product, program, etc. is officially available to purchase or sign up for.

Instead of Searching for the "Right" Idea, Ask Good Questions

- ★ What's a problem people tend to ask me to help solve?
- ★ What have I walked through that others are still struggling with currently?
- ★ What could I talk about for hours and not get bored?
- ★ What's a problem I *want* to help solve?
- ★ What skills, lived experiences, or obsessions do I already have?

This isn't about being the most qualified. It's about starting where your energy naturally wants to go.

What I Needed Became My Business

When I first started offering online coaching services, my focus was around self-care, which I had no formal training in, it is not what my PhD is in or what I studied in school, and is definitely not what I do now in my business as I'm writing this eight years after starting. At the time, I was the mom of a kindergartner and two teens. I was also a full-time English professor and had a small part-time massage practice. I'm now divorced, but back then, my marriage was becoming not-so-healthy, *and* we were in the throes of moving into a 1924 home that needed some work. In addition, I felt completely disconnected from my body, and you might see why self-care became important to me. I invested in myself by hiring my first coach, the amazing Carly Clark Zimmer, and began rediscovering who I was, what my values were, how to hold boundaries for those values, and how to integrate self-care on the daily that supported a growing reconnection to myself. As a massage therapist then, it was quite natural for me to share things with my clients that would help them between massage sessions. I was also sharing things about my self-care journey online and got a few comments here and there. I was noticing more and more of my female friends getting curious about what I was doing to help myself. Because many of them did not live in my town, and therefore couldn't come get a massage from me, I got curious about how I might support these women from afar. That's when I started offering my "Fundamentals of Self-Care" customized one-on-one program. I didn't know exactly what I was doing, but it just felt good to help women find their own small shifts that would support them in filling their cups first. To be honest, I struggled because the work with my first few clients in this program felt "easy." One thing you will discover as you embark on your entrepreneurial journey is that letting it be *easy* and receiving for that (aka getting paid and not overworking) will be one of your greatest challenges. I was not, and am still not, an expert in self-care and prioritizing myself as a mom and woman. But, because I was seeing huge and powerful transformations in my life as I learned to take care of myself in deep ways, it was a natural first step and offer for my online business. My business has shifted so much since then, but I still carry tenets from those early days, and I am grateful for that experience. So, go back to the questions shared previously and see what shows up! Next, I'll share some simple ways to get started, let it be messy, and do what comes easy … which is often easier said than done!

Idea Clarity = Action Clarity

You will not think your way into a perfect business. You will test, tweak, and *feel* your way into clarity.

Try this, and of course write it down:

1. **Pick one idea.** Not five. One. Let it be the one that feels "too easy."
2. **Commit to experimenting with it for 90 days.**
3. **Make a messy offer around it.** See what happens.
4. **Track what lights you up and what drains you.**
5. **Let the path unfold through doing, not just dreaming.**

You are allowed to pivot.
You are allowed to change your mind.
You just have to *start* so there's something to grow.

Real Talk for the Overthinker

If you're waiting for "certainty" before you begin, you'll be waiting forever. Certainty is a byproduct of movement—not a prerequisite.

Read that again.

Indecision does not build businesses. At some point, you have to put the Pinterest board down and say:

"F*ck it—I'm trying this."

Clarity doesn't come from asking the Internet. It comes from asking your *intuition*—and then listening long enough to hear what it says.

Final Words

The idea you start with won't be the one you scale with.
The offer you put out first might bomb.
The confidence won't arrive before you begin—it'll meet you on the road.

But you? You're exactly where you need to be.
Wrestling with doubt. Daring to dream.
Standing at the edge of something real.

Start where you are.
With what you know.
And build from there.

Clarity comes through action, not perfection.

CHAPTER 2

You Will Cry in Your Sweatpants

AND WHY THIS IS TOTALLY NORMAL

Real Talk

Starting a business is not just a financial or strategic decision. It's an emotional initiation.

It will crack you open.

It will bring up alllll your stuff.

And sometimes, it will break you down at 2am while you're still in last night's sweats, questioning every decision you've ever made.

This chapter isn't to scare you. It's here to prepare you.

I have been right where you are right now, and I'm here to tell you that not only can you do this, but you must. If you are feeling the entrepreneurial tug, if something is pulling you forward to share your gifts with the world, to work differently, to honor your values, then know that tug is there for a reason. You must always come back to this tug and you must always trust it, whether you are on a loving sales call with an amazing new client or in last night's sweats crying on the couch because it seems like no one wants to work with you.

What No One Tells You About the Emotional Ride

Starting a business is not a linear process. It is a roller coaster of both/and experiences over and over (and *over*) again.

- ★ You will feel like a genius *and* a failure in the same week.
- ★ You'll compare your Day 1 to someone else's Year 5 *and* wonder if you're cut out for this.
- ★ People you love won't "get it"—*and* that will sting more than you expect.
- ★ You'll try to make your first $500 *and* somehow end up in a 3-day spiral about your worth.
- ★ You'll be told "just be consistent" *and* want to throw your laptop across the room.

And still—you'll keep going.

Why It Feels So Personal

Here's the thing: you are not just selling a product or service. You're putting *your ideas, voice, values, creativity, and time* on the line.

Starting a business asks you to:

- ★ Be seen
- ★ Take up space
- ★ Make decisions without guarantees
- ★ Risk rejection (and eventually learn to value the "no's")
- ★ Believe in something *before* you have the evidence

That's not small. That's sacred. And yes—sometimes excruciating. One of the most important things I have learned is to understand the both/and of *expansion* and *contraction* in running a business.

Becoming Comfortable with the Uncomfortable

When you start your business, when you finally say YES to this tug, hope, dream, desire, it will feel amazingly expansive! Think of how it will feel (or felt) when you get your first client. The possibilities feel endless when you actually get to support someone or share what you created ... and get paid for it. These moments of expansion are important! Write them down as *receipts*, aka reminders and proof, that you can do this and that you are doing this.

I will never forget my first coaching client! I was still teaching full-time and had started a very small massage practice business when I discovered life coaching. I watched an inspiring webinar online (thank you, Laura Wieck, for saying yes and following the tug for your business, BodyMind Coaching™), and the wheels started churning. I created an offer that combined massage with life coaching. Because of my background in teaching, I knew how to design a curriculum or a plan for someone to help them go from Point A to Point B. I created this very simple, but way too detailed, program description and offered it to five of my best, most loyal current clients. To my surprise, the one who said "yes," and paid in full for my $2600 six-month program of coaching and massage, was someone I never thought I'd work with. He was a retired veteran. And while he certainly was familiar with dealing with bodily injuries over the years because of his time in combat, he was not as familiar with really tuning in and listening to his body, his breath. Working with him felt like my wink from the Divine, the Universe that I was on the right path. The feeling of expansion, of taking up space, and of being seen and affirmed was intoxicating in all the best ways. But much like a rubber band, expansion has a limit in the moment. A rubber band, at a certain point and size, can only stretch and expand so far or it will snap. Our journey in business is no different.

Immediately following enrolling my new client, I had several other people I had made my offer to tell me "no." And not just a simple "no," but more like a "Who do you think you are asking people to pay that much for XYZ, helllll no." On the heels of my first big *yes*, I fell into deep discomfort and began questioning myself and what I was doing in starting this business. I completely forgot about my amazing new client! Enter *contraction*. While I don't want you to expect contractions to happen or to be waiting for the other shoe to drop after a moment of expansion or an exciting sale, it is important to know that moments of contraction, doubt, fear, and questioning are normal. When they happen, know that nothing has gone wrong. You are simply making room for the next level of expansion, dreaming, goal-ing, and simply making room for more of what you desire to show up. It's hard to believe, but where you are now will not be where you are in a month, six months, or a year from now. Next, I share some ways to help navigate the emotional rollercoaster ride of expansion and contraction as an entrepreneur. Becoming comfortable with the uncomfortable will soon be your new superpower!

Mantras for the Messy Middle

Use these. Tape them to your mirror. Tattoo them on your heart.

- ★ "It's okay to feel like a mess and still be making magic."
- ★ "This is hard because it matters—not because I'm doing it wrong."
- ★ "Clarity comes through action, not perfection."
- ★ "Other people's doubt doesn't mean your dream is wrong."
- ★ "My nervous system needs care, not shame."

What to Do When You're Spiraling

When the crying-on-the-couch moment hits (because it will), try this:

1. **Name It.**
   → "I'm overwhelmed because this is new, not because I'm failing."
2. **Move It.**
   → Dance it out. Go on a rage walk. Cry in the shower. Feel it fully. Then keep going.
3. **Zoom Out.**
   → Look at how far you've come—even if you've just started.
4. **Call In Support.**
   → Talk to another entrepreneur. Make sure you hire a coach, mentor, join a community, etc. Most people *won't* understand, but your people do exist, and you will need them.
5. **Re-anchor to your why.**
   → Not the surface "I want to make money" one. The deeper one. The one that makes your throat tight.

Final Words

If you're in the hard part right now, please know this:

You're not broken.
You're not behind.
You're building something real.

Crying in your sweatpants doesn't mean you're failing.

It means you care.
It means you're stretching.
It means you're becoming someone who can hold
what they're creating.

Keep going.
Even with puffy eyes.

Fear is going to be on the ride with you. It just doesn't get to drive the bus.

CHAPTER 3

Making Offers Without Feeling Gross About It

―――――――――――

BECAUSE SALES IS LOVE

―――――――――――

Let's Talk About the "S" Word: Sales

Just reading that word probably made something in your body clench. Sales? Ew. Cringe. That's for bro-marketers and corporate robots, right?

Not quite.

If you're here, you probably:

* ★ Want to help people
* ★ Believe deeply in your work
* ★ Care about connection, authenticity, and values
* ★ Suffered trauma related to sales, manipulation, or pressure tactics.

So when it comes time to *make an offer*, you feel like you're betraying your integrity—even though you're literally trying to help someone.

Let's clear that up.

A Reframe That Changes Everything

Selling is just inviting someone into transformation.

That's it. My long-time business coach and sales goddess, Laura Wright, says, "Sales is love." Radical? I know! But if you have no sales, if you aren't inviting people to work with you or buy your products, then you don't have a business. You are also depriving both yourself and others of benefiting from the gifts you can offer the world.

So, reframing sales is stepping into a conversation with someone and saying:

- ★ "Here's something I created to support you."
- ★ "Here's how it works, what it costs, and how to join."
- ★ "Here's why I believe it can help."

You're not convincing anyone. You're not tricking anyone. You're just offering something real—to someone who might need it.

Why We Struggle with Making Offers

Let's name what's underneath the fear of selling:

- ★ "I don't want to be pushy."
- ★ "I don't want people to think I'm just doing this for money."
- ★ "I'm afraid they'll say no, and I'll take it personally."
- ★ "I don't want to annoy people or get unfollowed."
- ★ "I feel like I have to be someone else to do this right."

You're not alone.

But here's the truth: The world doesn't need more polished pitches. It needs more people saying real things about what they offer—and why it matters.

You Don't Have to Use Sleazy Tactics

Let's be clear about what you **don't** need to do:

- ★ Use fake scarcity ("Only 2 spots left!" when you'd take 10)
- ★ Promise life-changing results if you haven't seen them yet
- ★ Cold DM strangers pretending you "love their vibe"
- ★ Act like your offer is the only path to success
- ★ Pretend you have it all figured out

People can smell performative marketing from a mile away. But they also *feel* it when you're being real.

What to Do Instead: Selling Like a Human

Here's what actually works (and feels good):

1. **Have a conversation.**
   While it is possible to make click-to-buy sales, especially for products and low-ticket offers (ex. $500 or less), the best pathway to learning how to sell is by simply talking to people, listening with the intent to understand their needs and struggles, and only making an offer if you feel like what you do can actually support them.
2. **Lead with service.**
   Talk about the problem you solve and how you help—not just the price and the features.

3. **Tell the story.**
   Share *why* you created this offer. What led you here? What did you wish you had when you were struggling? Telling your authentic story is super powerful.
4. **Speak to one person.**
   Don't try to convince the masses. In your posts, emails, videos, and conversations, speak to the one person who's secretly hoping someone gets it.
5. **Be clear, not clever.**
   Tell people what you're offering, who it's for, how it works, and how to sign up. Period.
6. **Repeat yourself.**
   People need to hear about something multiple times before it clicks. Though it will feel annoying, it's not—it's building connection.

"But What If They Say No?"

They will. Sometimes often. And guess what? That's okay.

A no isn't a personal rejection. It's clarity. It means someone *wasn't ready, wasn't a fit,* or *just wasn't the one you're here to help.*

You are not here to be chosen by everyone. You are here to stand in your truth—and let the right ones lean in.

Seeking Alignment Over a Yes
Learning who you are *not* a fit for is probably one

of the most powerful things you can discover when starting your online business. Learning to value a no is just as important as celebrating a yes! This took me a while to learn. In my fourth year in business, I enrolled a new client in a six-month coaching program. The new client had been referred to me by one of my current clients, which felt like a good sign since the current client was amazing to work with (almost all of my business is through referrals and connections now). I scheduled the discovery call (aka sales call), and listened as this potential client shared everything she was struggling with. I had experienced enough of these calls that I could hear the distinct indicators that her struggles were definitely something that my support could help her with. But there was one problem: the energy on the call was extremely low and pessimistic. While I am not what I would consider a "peppy all the time" kind of person, I am passionate and try to find the beauty in life, even when it totally sucks in the moment. I noticed some word choices showing that while this potential client was clearly struggling, she was not interested in actual change.

Even though I could tell she was likely not very coachable, she liked what I offered, and I decided that gaining a new client and bringing in more income was more important than my gut instinct that felt we were likely not a good fit to work together. And off we went, diving right into the program. I quickly confirmed my gut instincts as the client was often late for her coaching sessions, and one time did not even show up! She struggled to take action with her plans she created with my guidance and knew would help her get meaningful results on her goals. After two months, I scheduled a call with her, and we mutually agreed that our work together was not in alignment, releasing her from the program. I felt the biggest sigh of relief! Was this experience uncomfortable? Hell yes! Did I learn a ton about listening for alignment, as well as trusting when I felt that lack of alignment, on a sales call? Double hell yes!

A no is just as important as a yes. Learning to accept them both as a part of the online business journey is key!

Something to Help You Start

Not sure how to talk about your offer in online spaces? Take this starter language, adapt it, add to it, take out what you don't like, and see what feels good for you:

> "I made something I'm really proud of. It's for [the person you help] who's dealing with [their struggle or desire]. Inside, we focus on [what it includes or delivers]. Who do you know that might love this? DM me or check the link in my bio to learn more."

Simple. Honest. No ick. The more you can get in your authenticity and simply state your offer and how to get started, the more authentic sales will feel. Michelle Rockwood, author of *Joyful Selling*, gifted me this phrasing: "The grass is green, the sky is blue, I'm Shana, and I help people write and share powerful messages in books. Would you like to learn more?"

Boom. How can it be just that easy? Now go practice!

Final Words

You don't need to become someone else to make an offer.

You just need to believe in what you've built—and speak to the people who are already looking for it. Remember ...

Selling isn't about pushing.
It's about presenting.
It's about holding your offer with open hands, not grabbing fists.
It's about sharing from your values, not your fear.

So go ahead and tell them what you made. The people who need it are waiting. Not for perfection— but for you. As my good friend and mentor, Laura Wieck, always says, "Remember, you are the gift!"

You were not born to work for free.

CHAPTER 4

Getting Paid Without Selling Your Soul

DIVING INTO THE UNCOMFORTABLE ART OF RECEIVING

The Elephant in the Room

We all have money stories. They may be good and healthy. They may be terrible and unhelpful. But we all have them. This is why starting an online business and charging for your work can feel ... weird as hell.

You want to help people. You believe in your offer, services, or product. You *know* it can change lives.

But the moment you have to put a **price tag** on it?

Cue the existential crisis:

- ★ "Is this too much?"
- ★ "What if no one buys?"
- ★ "Who do I think I am?"
- ★ "Maybe I should just offer it for free until I build confidence ..."

STOP.

Let's get one thing clear before we go any further:

> Being well-compensated for your work
> is not a betrayal of your values.

It's an *embodiment* of them.

Why Does Pricing Feel So Personal?

Because it *is*. Especially if:

- ★ You're a first-generation entrepreneur
- ★ You received messages growing up like "money doesn't grow on trees" or "don't ask for too much"
- ★ You're a helper, healer, or creative
- ★ You're still learning how to feel safe being seen and celebrated

You've likely learned that:

- ★ Money is dirty
- ★ Selling is selfish
- ★ Wanting "more" makes you greedy
- ★ You should give it all away and be grateful for what you have

So when you start a business—especially a heart-centered one—you bump into all of that.

Therefore, pricing isn't just a business decision. It's an emotional reckoning.

Reframing What You're Actually Selling

You're not selling your soul.
You're not selling your worth.
You're not selling out.

You're offering someone a path, a solution, a shift.

You're charging for:

★ Your time
★ Your energy
★ Your skills
★ Your lived experience
★ Your capacity to hold space and lead people through transformation

Your price reflects the *value of the result*, not the value of **you**.

Let that land. Seriously: pause, reflect, write.

I'll say it again: Your price reflects the *value of the result*, not the value of **you**.

Pricing Without Panic

Here's a better way to approach pricing. Do some writing around the following questions and make sure you add numbers when prompted (marked by a $).

Step 1: Anchor the transformation
★ What result or experience are you helping someone create or move through?
★ What is the value of this transformation? $ _____
★ What is the cost of someone staying stuck/not making any change? $ _____ (think of all the ways we numb, distract, make ourselves feel better in temporary and superficial ways)

Step 2: Check your energy & genuine needs

- ★ What do you need to make on a monthly/yearly basis to make sure you and your family are taken care of? $ _____
- ★ What do you want to make on a monthly/ yearly basis to go beyond basic needs and into a feeling of abundance? $ _____
- ★ Does the price of your offer feel like a fair exchange—or does it leave you depleted or resentful and not actually allow you to receive what you need and want?

Step 3: Consider your capacity

- ★ How many people can you serve at this level sustainably?
- ★ Think about your energy, needs, and desires in Step 2. Then, play with different numbers of clients and pricing to help you meet your income goals.

Step 4: Give yourself permission to evolve

- ★ Your first price isn't your forever price. You get to adjust.
- ★ How many people are you comfortable enrolling at your current price? When would you love to change that price? What would you like to increase it to at that point? $ _____

From $49 to $50k

Remember how I first started my business as a massage therapist? When I began, I charged $49 for a one-hour massage. I remember going as low as $39 for a "special rate" at one point. Ya'll, let that sink in. $39 for using my energy, techniques, and training, which I certainly paid more than $39/hour to learn, for helping someone potentially feel better and healthier in their body. While I knew from the start that my little massage practice would not be my way out of academia, my full-time job, I was certainly not doing myself any favors toward what I was building: more freedom in my life. Luckily, this is not where I ended up by the time I was closing my massage practice and stepping fully into my coaching, writing support, and publishing business. I had more than doubled my rates in my massage practice, but it was a roller coaster journey to get there. And while my first ever coaching offer was $2600 for a six-month program, my very next coaching offer was for just $100/month. Slowly but surely, my pricing has shifted from fear and uncertainty to clarity and confidence. Remember, within three years of starting my online business, I was making $10k offers. I almost peed my pants when I said that number out loud for the first time! As I'm writing this book in 2025, I have had an online business for eight years, and the highest level of support my team and I offer starts at $50k. Notice how you are reacting as you read these numbers. Eight years ago Shana certainly wasn't "there" yet! I had to do some deep reflection, personal work, and receive much support around money and pricing my offers. In my experience, the question of "who am I to do this, offer this, receive at this level" doesn't really go away ... and that's whether your offer is $20 or $20,000, seriously! The number is not what matters, but rather how those numbers feel inside your heart and soul, along with the reality of what you need to bring in for income. Trust me when I say you will find what works now and feels aligned now, and it *will* change. And it should change! As you grow and learn, as you work with clients and they have amazing results, as you expand, so should the way you get paid.

Side Note: I realize I am sharing this big jump in numbers above without going into detail about exactly *how* I got there or tips on how you can get there. I'm intentionally leaving out the experience and expertise, the training and certifications, the coaching ... all of which were things I invested heavily in to support my journey. Mainly because your experience will also differ from mine. And this is what I support people in doing: finding their pathway to an aligned and abundant online business. I'd love to help you along the way. Jump to the end of the book for ways we can work together!

"But What If No One Buys at This Price?"

A genuine fear—and a real possibility. Here's what to know:

* Price isn't always the reason people don't buy. Sometimes it's clarity, timing, or trust.
* Underpricing doesn't guarantee sales. It often just brings in people who don't value the work.
* Your job isn't to make it affordable to *everyone*. Your job is to make it valuable to the *aligned* ones.

And when someone says, "I can't afford it," it doesn't mean:

- ★ You've done something wrong.
- ★ You should immediately drop your price.
- ★ You're too much.

It simply means it's not a fit right now. We all have stories around money, and I clarify that working with me and my team should never compromise one's well-being or livelihood. You may see a lot of bro-sales tactics online that talk about exposing "pain points" and using unethical tactics around pricing and sales, like guilt and shame. Yes, there are some tools and strategies that can be helpful that will work for you, but I always fall back on what Michelle Rockwood, sales coach, has reminded me many times: "I am just a girl on a call getting to know someone."

So stay grounded. Don't chase. Don't spiral. Part of the transformation happens when someone *decides* to invest in themselves, and you are so here for that!

The Art of Receiving

Okay, here's the real kicker: Even when the payment *does* come in, many people don't actually let themselves *receive it.*

You discount it. Downplay it. Say "thank you" with an awkward emoji and immediately start worrying if you're worth it.

Let's shift that:

Practice receiving like a damn CEO.

- ★ Pause.
- ★ Celebrate.
- ★ Feel gratitude.
- ★ Let it land.
- ★ Trust that more is coming.

Your nervous system might not be used to this yet—but you're building new pathways of safety around being seen, supported, and paid. And it's okay if it takes time.

Real Talk: Stop Justifying Your Worth

You don't need to:

- ★ List every single detail and deliverable of your offer to "prove" the price
- ★ Add more and more bonuses to make it "worth it"
- ★ Apologize for charging
- ★ Shrink your vision to make others more comfortable

You don't owe anyone a justification for valuing your labor. And anyone who makes you feel you do? Not your people.

Final Words

You were not born to work for free.

You were not born to stay small just because capitalism is loud and you're trying to do things with integrity.

You are allowed to be spiritual, ethical, creative, generous—and still want to build a business that *pays your bills and funds your dreams*. You are the person who will do great things with the way you receive! Remember …

> Receiving is not selfish.
> Being yourself is most aligned.
> Getting paid is not selling out.

It's your brave, rebellious act of reclaiming your power.

It's okay to feel like a mess and still be making magic.

CHAPTER 5

When It Feels Like No One Is Buying

LEANING AWAY FROM HUSTLE AND INTO
SHOWING UP AUTHENTICALLY

When You've Given It Your All ... and Hear Crickets

So, you made the thing. You poured your heart into it. Posted on Instagram. Maybe even a story or two with an animated text that said, "Link in bio!" You hit publish ... and waited.

And waited.
And waited.

... And no one bought it.

Cue the spiral:

- ★ "Do I suck at this?"
- ★ "Was my idea dumb?"
- ★ "Maybe I should just go back to [insert soul-sucking job here]."

Listen—this moment sucks. But it doesn't mean you're failing. It means you're learning how to market like an actual human. I actually don't even like to use the word "market/marketing." I prefer *connection*. Because as a heart-centered, mission-driven, genuine human, who cares about other humans, what you are really doing is trying to *connect* with your aligned people who have been hoping, wishing, praying for what you offer.

Why It Feels Like No One's Buying

Let's break it down, lovingly but honestly:

It's probably not that your offer is bad.

It's more likely that:

- ★ You're not talking about it enough (seriously—people need 7–20+ touchpoints).
- ★ You're blending in because you're afraid to take up space.
- ★ You're trying to do it all alone in a vacuum instead of leaning on and investing in community, feedback, and support.
- ★ You're making assumptions instead of having genuine conversations.
- ★ You launched … but didn't *sell*. (More on this in a second.)

Real Talk: You Can't DIY Your Way Through Every Block

Entrepreneurship can feel isolating, especially when you're staring at your laptop wondering if your Canva graphic is the reason no one clicked.

But this is not supposed to be a solo mission.

Here's what actually moves the needle:

- ★ Getting real feedback from people you trust (not just your cousin who "loves it!")
- ★ Asking your community what they *need*, not guessing
- ★ Reaching out to someone you've helped and saying: "Hey, who do you know that could really

use this kind of support?"
* Letting your work be visible, messy,
   and in-progress
* Investing in your own support—hiring a coach,
   joining a mastermind, shadowing a mentor, etc.

You don't have to "figure it out" by over-Googling or trying to reverse-engineer someone's sales funnel. Sometimes, you just need to say:

"Hey, I made this. Want to take a look?"

No pitch deck required.

Don't Underestimate Your Existing Network

Your first clients? They are probably not going to be strangers on the Internet.

They're your friend's cousin. That person from your book club. Someone who's been watching you for months but hasn't said a word—until you say, *"I'm open for business."*

We often ignore the people who already know, like, and trust us because we fear being *too much.* Or we don't want to "bother" them.

But here's a reframe:

You're not begging people to buy.
You're offering solutions to people who might actually need them.

You're simply making an invitation; people get to say yes or no.

Consider the people around you currently who might need what you are offering or may be connected to individuals who need what you are offering.

What You Don't Need to Do

You do **not** need to:

- ★ Create a 17-step funnel before you've sold one spot
- ★ Use urgency timers that make your skin crawl
- ★ Start TikTok, Threads, *and* a YouTube channel this week
- ★ Fake scarcity to make people buy faster
- ★ Lower your price out of fear
- ★ Outsource/hire someone to "do it for you" too soon

That Time I Tried to Skip Ahead

In the third year of my then self-care/personal growth coaching business, I started to really hit my stride. I had worked with several clients, and through those experiences and feedback, I fine-tuned my offer and loved how I was supporting my clients. I had just created and sold my first high-ticket program, a $10k year-long, customized 1:1 program. Amazing! This client was a classic "friend of a friend" referral, and she had done some smaller coaching program work with me first. We had had many conversations about stepping into this deep-level program before she actually said "yes."

Despite the pathway this high-level client came to work with me, I thought I was ready to skip ahead to the wild world of running ads and getting cold audience leads. I thought the best way to do that was to invest in running Facebook ads to my free Facebook group. I found an aligned and high-quality ads team to work with. The support was significant, and the ads "worked" in that we achieved our goal to bring more people into the Facebook group ... my thinking was more people would eventually equal more sales and clients whenever I made offers in that group. I know, I *know*! But here's the thing: not only were Facebook ads an investment, but I was also investing in the creating, optimizing, monitoring, and adjusting of those ads. That amazing $10,000 influx into my business that I got through authentic nurturing and many conversations? It was like I could not spend it fast enough, and it quickly dwindled. Also, I was investing a lot of money in getting folks into a *free* offer, the Facebook group. It worked in that my group grew to about 1,000 people with these new members. Then, I began nurturing these new members by running a *free* self-care challenge of sorts in the group. I showed up for days, going live, giving them lots of support, creating guides and handouts ... all for *free*. Then, imagine my shock when no one, not one person, bought my new group program that was about $500/month, something I had also spent tons of time developing. More people did not in fact, equal more clients. Free offers did not, in fact, lead to paying clients. Outsourcing did not, in fact, lead to growth.

I learned a lot from this experience. While I can certainly now see what I would do differently, I needed to go through this experience to understand important things like:

- ★ People who want "free" things will often always want "free" things
- ★ You don't need a large audience to sell your high-ticket offer
- ★ Scaling may not be your business model. And that's okay.
- ★ Talk to people. Talk to people. Talk to people.
- ★ Sales calls and conversations first over ads and fancy funnels

Starting your business and selling isn't about tricks. It's about trust. You build trust when you show up, speak authentically, and keep showing up, even when it is quiet.

Rebuilding Momentum Without Burnout

Try this when it feels like no one's buying:

1. **Ask yourself honestly:** Did I *really* talk about it enough—or just post once, cross my fingers, and hope?
2. **Look at your offer:** Is it solving a problem someone would pay to solve? (Not just something you love to talk about?)
3. **Talk to real humans:** Ask past clients, friends, followers, potential clients: "What are you struggling with lately?"
4. **Simplify your strategy:** Focus on one offer, one audience, one platform—for now.

5. **Call in support:** Hire a coach. Join a community. Ask a biz friend to co-work with you. You're not weak for needing help—you're smart for not wasting time in the dark.
6. **Take care of yourself**: Be sure to keep doing the things that keep you grounded and sane … sacred morning time, walking the dog, time with your friends and family, fun night out!

Final Words

When it feels like no one's buying, the instinct is to shrink. To make yourself smaller. To back away and pretend this whole business thing didn't matter, anyway.

But here's the truth: Your work deserves to be seen.

You are allowed to be proud of what you made. And someone out there is quietly waiting for the exact thing you're afraid to share again.

So get loud.
Get visible.
And get supported.

You don't need a trick. You need *a connection*.
You don't need to do it all. You need a *circle*.
You don't need a perfect plan. You just need to *keep going*.

Even if it's quiet. Even if no one buys today. Your work still matters.

You're not
behind. You're
building
something real.

Visibility Gut-Check Worksheet

BEFORE YOU DECIDE YOUR OFFER IS DOOMED,
CHECK IN WITH THE FACTS—NOT YOUR FEARS.

Am I Actually Talking About My Offer?

○ I've clearly shared what I'm offering at least ____ times in the past seven days.

○ I've explained who it's for and what it helps with (not just "I'm so excited!!").

○ I've used both stories and clear info to make it real for people.

○ I've made it easy for people to find the link or next step (like a sales call).

○ I've followed up with people who were "interested" (without ghosting out of fear).

○ I've asked a few trusted people for honest feedback on how I'm explaining it.

NOTES

What am I noticing?

_____

_____

_____

What could be clearer or more direct?

_____

_____

_____

What would feel really aligned and supportive?

_____

_____

_____

Am I Hiding Without Realizing It?

- ○ I posted once and hoped people would "just know" it was for them.
- ○ I didn't mention the offer in my stories, emails, or conversations this week.
- ○ I was afraid of being annoying, so I stayed vague.
- ○ I focused more on Canva colors than connection.
- ○ I convinced myself no one wanted it … without talking to anyone.
- ○ I didn't tap into my existing network because I didn't want to be "that person."

NOTES

What's one bold thing I could do this week to stop hiding?

_____

_____

_____

Energy & Alignment Check

How does this offer actually feel in my body?

○ I'm excited to share it
○ I feel unsure or disconnected
○ I'm exhausted just thinking about it

What's fueling this offer right now?

○ Passion + purpose
○ Pressure + panic
○ A little of both

NOTES

What part of this offer lights me up?

_____

_____

_____

What part needs a shift or simplification?

_____

_____

_____

Would I invest in this offer? How would it support me (now or in the past)?

_____

_____

_____

What's One Simple Step I Can Take Today?

Instead of doing *everything*, what's **one small action** I can take to build trust and visibility today?

Example prompts (Note: these can be done via email, social media, in a Zoom call, and/or over coffee):

- ★ Share a behind-the-scenes story
- ★ Talk about why I made this offer
- ★ DM someone who's shown interest
- ★ Re-post a testimonial or kind word
- ★ Go live and share my heart
- ★ Ask my audience a question related to the offer

MY ONE STEP TODAY

_____

_____

_____

CHAPTER 6

Fear of Being Seen

AND HOW TO SHOW UP ANYWAY

The Part No One Puts in Their Polished Carousel Posts

Visibility is terrifying.

Not just scary in the "what if no one buys" kind of way—but in the **"oh god, what if people actually** see **me?"** way. What if people actually ...

- ★ See my weird ideas?
- ★ See my typos?
- ★ See me stumble through a launch?
- ★ See me try and *still* not succeed right away?

If you feel your stomach tighten when you go to post something vulnerable, promote your offer, or follow up with that potential client, *you are not broken*. You are human.

And if you've felt massive resistance to showing your face, sharing your voice, or being more open online ... That's not a marketing problem. That's a very real, very normal nervous system response. And we can learn to work with our fears ... promise!

Visibility ≠ Safety (At Least, Not at First)

Here's the truth: putting yourself out there *can* feel like a threat—especially if:

- ★ Someone taught you not to take up too much space.
- ★ You were punished or criticized for expressing yourself.

★ You've had a lived experience where being "too visible" wasn't safe

No amount of business strategy will fix that if you don't also tend to the parts of you that feel *scared*. You can't mindset your way out of fear, but you *can* learn to move with it.

See, fear shows up as a mechanism to keep us safe. But, if you are at all familiar with the idea of your comfort zone, you'll quickly realize that starting a business will feel way, wayyyyy outside of your comfort zone. So, fear shows up to tell your body to "whoa down" and make sure there are no saber-tooth tigers on the other side of that email you are about to send, finally telling people your business is open. Yet, safety rarely equals success or following our dreams.

The Fear Will Come With You (But It Doesn't Get to Drive)

There's a thing I tell my clients all the time:

"Fear is going to be on the ride with you. It just doesn't get to drive the bus."

Trying to erase fear before you show up online is like trying to wait for "the perfect time" to start your business. It's not coming.

Instead, you need tools to help your body understand: "This is new, not dangerous."

So here's what that can actually look like …

Visibility Tools That Aren't Just "Post More"

★ **Before you post, ground yourself.**
Hand on your heart. Feet on the floor. Take three
deep breaths. Remind your body: I am safe to be
seen today.

★ **Name the fear.**
Write down what you're *actually* afraid will
happen. Will someone roll their eyes? Will your
uncle call it a pyramid scheme? Get it out of
your head and into the light.

★ **Start small.**
You don't have to go full TED Talk on Day 1. Try
a soft selfie. Share a sentence that feels true.
Let your nervous system acclimate to being
witnessed and "out there."

★ **Create safety in connection.**
Tell a biz bestie when you're about to post
something vulnerable. Visibility is less
scary when someone is clapping for you in
the comments.

★ **Let it be imperfect.**
Done is better than performative or super
polished. People don't connect with your
perfection; they connect with your truth.

Embracing and Embodying Fear
Fear is a compass.
Do it scared.
Fear is just part of the process.

I know these common catch phrases all too well, and they have never quite sat right with me. I think it's because I recognize that while mindset shifts and positive affirmations are an important part of any online business owner's journey, mindset alone will only get you so far. We *feel* fear.

When fear shows up, our body's response can vary from increased heart rate to sweaty palms to a pit in our stomach. Sometimes these catchphrases, while well-intentioned, cause us to bypass important sensations and feelings *in the body*. As a business owner, I have found that one of my biggest "jobs" is to sit in discomfort, fully feeling the fear (and anything else showing up), without bypassing or forcing myself to shift out of it quickly. I learn this lesson over and over and over again. Every time I share a new offer or an upcoming retreat or what feels like a bold, no f**cks to give post, fear shows up. Even though I have written and published many articles and books over the years, I almost changed the publishing date for my book *Writing Is Not That Hard: Empowering the Writer Within*. Why? Because it felt like I was taking my baby (okay, *book baby*) and sending it off into the world having zero idea if it would survive, if people would like it, and if it would actually help anyone. The fear was raging inside me. I grabbed my bodymind tools, which consisted of a lot of quiet time, word vomit journal writing, sharing with my writing buddy and business partner (love you, Cindy!), and even giving myself permission to push the publishing date back if I really was not ready. I call this "sinking all the way down to the bottom," letting myself really feel into all the potential worst-case scenarios, trusting that I could figure it out *if* anything not-so-great actually happened after the book was out.

Fast forward to the release date going off without a hitch, the book hitting *#1 Bestseller* on Amazon in several categories, and fear being present for the entire ride! There is no solution or *one right way* to overcome fear, at least none that I have found. Yet, the sooner you can find tools and ways of working *with* the fear, often the quicker fear will dissipate and you realize you've actually got this!

Final Words

There are people—right now—who are waiting for someone *exactly like you* to say the thing that gives them permission to try.

You don't have to shout that thing loudly to be seen. You don't have to be "on brand" 24/7. You just have to be *real*. That's what resonates.

So if you're feeling scared, anxious, or even nauseous before you show up? That's not a sign to shrink. It's a sign you're stretching.

And you're not doing it wrong—you're doing it *bravely*.

Receiving is
not selfish.
Getting paid is
not selling out.

CHAPTER 7

Navigating the Comparison
Spiral on Social Media

AND TRUSTING YOUR OWN DAMN PATH

Does This Sound Familiar?

You log onto Instagram, just wanting to post your "new offer is live!" story slide. Thirty minutes later, you're spiraling in a sea of:

- ★ Six-figure launch confetti graphics
- ★ Perfectly edited videos of someone's "slow CEO morning"
- ★ A reel of someone who "accidentally made $20k while napping"

Meanwhile, you're eating peanut butter off a spoon in your pajamas, wondering if you should just delete your entire account and move to the woods.

Welcome to the comparison spiral.

Your Brain Wasn't Built for This Many People Doing This Many Things

Social media is a highlight reel.
Yes, you know this logically.
But emotionally? It hits differently.

We're not just seeing one person doing well—we're seeing *hundreds* of people sharing wins, polished content, glowing testimonials, and launch day countdowns, all at once. Our brains scramble.

"She started after me and has 10k followers …"
"Should I be using that funnel strategy too?"

"Maybe I need better branding, a VA[3], a better website ..."

And suddenly, we're not *building* our business—we're benchmarking it against every single person we follow. No wonder it feels like you're always behind.

The Comparison Trap Is Not a Sign You're Failing

It's a sign you're human. It's also a sign that something deeper might need your attention.

Comparison usually shows up when you're:

★ Tired
★ Disconnected from your *why*
★ Over-consuming and under-creating
★ Operating from scarcity instead of trust

What we don't realize is that comparison often stems from a deeper issue of the systems, like social media and capitalism, that often are set up to keep us thinking we don't have enough of something (education, experience, money, material things, followers, etc.). Such systems keep us spiraling in the inner dialogue of "It's me. Hi. I'm the problem, it's me." (No shade on Taylor Swift!)

---

3. VA stands for "virtual assistant," which is someone who works for/with you like an in-person assistant might just virtually and usually asynchronously, assisting you with anything from personal tasks (like online grocery shopping) to business tasks (like email automations).

Why I Will Never Use the Term Imposter Syndrome Again

You may be reading this part of the book thinking, "But Shana, what about imposter syndrome? I know that's real because I feel it often!" Grab that spoon of peanut butter and your coziest spot on the couch for this one because I have got things to say!

A few years ago, when Synergy Publishing Group was really starting to take off and we were working with amazing clients to get their books out in the world, I started noticing the term "imposter syndrome" coming up over and over. I'd usually hear our clients mention it after they had written a good many pages and actually started to realize their book writing and publishing dreams could come true. Cue *imposter syndrome* voices ...

> *I like what I have written, but who would even want to read this?*
>
> *I think I may need to get some more experience, do some more research on ____ since it's a big part of my book (insert subject or concept or theme in their book). I don't think I am qualified enough yet to put this in my book.*
>
> *I'm not ____ (insert "famous" author, business person, etc.), so I'm not sure my ideas about this or my story even matters.*

Here's the thing: imposter syndrome is not new. The term has roots in psychology, particularly starting around the 1970s when psychologists began studying the clear gaps in women's achievements and abilities and their actual belief in themselves and those achievements and abilities. Most people use the term to refer to a feeling of lack in themselves, especially when comparing themselves to others, and these studies confirmed that the phenomenon often is positioned as an issue with the individual, something each person needs to solve for *themselves*. What we must realize, though, is that there are actual systemic issues that keep certain groups feeling a certain way about themselves. As one article shares, "Critics challenge this narrow focus, suggesting that [imposter syndrome] is a 'red herring,' diverting attention away from structural inequalities and problematic sociocultural values that may influence perceptions of inadequacy."[4] And this is why I try to avoid using the term when I'm in a comparison spiral! I now recognize that the issue is more so with the inherent dynamics of spaces like social media that push certain content this way and that with their algorithms. Something that I have little control over and that has no indication of something lacking in me or my abilities as a business owner. The trick isn't to *never* compare (good luck with that), but to actually understand what is happening, notice the spiral early, and interrupt it *with intention*. Let's work on that now!

---

4. LaDonna, K. A., Cowley, L., Field, E., Ginsburg, S., Watling, C., & Pack, R. (2025). Introducing the intruder paradox: "It's not the imposter syndrome, it's you don't want me in the field". *Medical education*, *59*(10), 1058–1066. https://doi.org/10.1111/medu.15741

Try This: A Comparison Spiral Interrupt

Here's a simple tool to help you unhook when the scroll turns into self-doubt:

Step 1: Pause and name what's happening.

"Oh. I'm comparing again. Got it."

Step 2: Ask yourself:

What story am I telling myself about this person's success?
What part of me feels activated right now?

Step 3: Reconnect to your own lane.

What am I working toward right now?
What do I actually want?
Is what they're doing even aligned with my vision?

Step 4: Close the app.

Seriously. Just log off. Go outside. Put your feet on the earth. Come back to yourself.

You Can Curate Your Feed Like a Grown-Ass CEO

You don't have to keep following people who leave you feeling small, less-than, or stuck in your head.

Try this mini-audit:

- ★ **Expanders:** Follow people who stretch you without making you feel like sh*t.
- ★ **Educators:** Follow folks who *teach* you, not just sell to you.
- ★ **Peers:** Stay connected to other actual humans on the journey—not just the gurus.
- ★ Unfollow or mute anyone who triggers performative pressure or shame. That includes people you "used to admire."

You're allowed to curate an online experience that supports your nervous system *and* your business.

Your Business Is Not Behind

There is no rulebook. No timeline. No exact number of reels to post or launches to do before you've "made it."

If someone is ahead of you, it's only because they're on a *different path*.

And here's the kicker: most of the people you're comparing yourself to?

They're comparing themselves to someone else, too.

The Reframe

Next time you see someone "ahead" of you online, try saying:

"That's what's possible when you stay the course."

Their success isn't a threat. It's proof.
Proof that showing up works.
That offers get traction.
That audiences grow.

If it's possible for them, it's possible for you—*in your own time, in your own way*.

Final Words

Comparison is natural—but it doesn't have to steal your joy, sabotage your creativity, or make you question your enough-ness.

The goal isn't to bypass it. It's to *navigate* it.

Come back to your own body. Your own wisdom. Your own why. No one else can build *your* business. No one else can say it the way *you* would.

And remember: no one's posting about the hard days. The tears. The awkward live stream that no one watched. The four "likes" on a heartfelt post.

You're not behind. You're just seeing everyone else's edited version of reality.

Keep showing up as the unfiltered version of yourself.

You don't need
to become
someone
else to share
your business.

CHAPTER 8

How to Seem Like a Pro

BEFORE YOU ACTUALLY FEEL LIKE ONE

What Professionalism Really Means

Spoiler: Professionalism isn't about fancy software, perfect branding, or having a 42-step automated funnel. It's about follow-through, communication, and clarity. Period.

When I started my online business, I felt anything *but* professional. I was piecing things together with free tools, working from my dining room table, and still occasionally had Goldfish crumbs stuck to my laptop keyboard (thanks, kids). But you know what? My clients didn't care. What they cared about was how I made them feel, how clearly I communicated, and whether I did what I said I was going to do.

So if you're feeling like you can't "go pro" until you've got a custom website, client management system, business cards, branded stationery, and a personal assistant named Sage who lights your palo santo candle for you each morning … slow your roll.

Here's how to show up like a pro, even while you're figuring it all out …

Follow Up (The #1 Easiest Thing You Can Do to Stand Out)

You'd be shocked—*shocked*—at how many people just don't follow up. Someone expresses interest, and then *crickets*. Or someone asks a question and never gets an answer. Or worse, a potential client says, "Yes, I'd love to work with you," and they never receive the next step to actually pay or get started.

Friend, don't let this be you.

Create a simple follow-up system. That might be:

- ★ A sticky note or Trello board
- ★ A spreadsheet with names and next steps
- ★ A recurring calendar reminder
- ★ A Gmail star system

It doesn't need to be fancy, but it needs to exist. Follow up with people. Get back to them when you say you will. Thank them for their interest. If someone expresses a "maybe," schedule a follow up date, give them some homework they can do in the meantime to come to an aligned decision, and then circle back as agreed upon. That alone will put you ahead of 90% of online business owners. Heck, this will put you ahead of most business owners!

Say What You Do (and Don't) Do

Nothing builds trust faster than transparency. You don't need to offer everything to everyone. In fact, please don't. Instead, be clear about what's in your wheelhouse—and what's not.

Someone asks for something outside your scope? Say:

"That's not something I specialize in, but I know someone who might be a better fit. Want me to send you their info?"

Boom. Professional. Generous. Clear. And a great way to potentially earn commissions from referrals!

You are allowed to have boundaries in business *and* still be wildly helpful and kind. People remember that.

Set Yourself Up to Get Paid Easily

The moment someone says, "I'm in!" is the moment you support their decision by taking payment. I suggest doing this on the spot with them if you are on a Zoom call, but you can also send them the link to pay or schedule or sign up. Don't wait. Don't make them chase you. Don't overcomplicate it with twelve emails and a customized welcome kit you're still designing.

Use simple tools:

- ★ Stripe (my go-to), Square, Venmo (depending on your industry and location)
- ★ PayPal
- ★ Google Forms for intake
- ★ Google Docs for onboarding
- ★ Calendly or Acuity for scheduling

You can always refine and upgrade later. For now, keep it simple and keep the energy moving.

Use Free Tools to Stay Organized

No one expects a fully customized online dashboard or a high-end client portal right out of the gate (unless you're building that for other people, in which case, rock on). But having *some* system in place for staying organized—especially with client info—is key.

Start with:

- Google Drive: Keep yourself organized by client/project. Share folders if needed.
- Gmail + labels: Keep communication searchable and tidy.
- Google Docs: For notes, agreements, shared outlines, whatever. (You can even collect signatures via the Drawing feature)
- A shared calendar: for scheduling sessions or deadlines.

Is this glamorous? No. Is it effective? Absolutely.

Do What You Say You'll Do

This is the whole damn secret to achieving pro status. If you say you'll email the intake form today, do it. If you say you'll send the next steps by Friday, send them by Friday.

And when life happens (because it will), don't ghost. Communicate. Be honest. Tell them what shifted, when they can expect to hear from you, and apologize if needed.

Most people don't need perfection. They just want communication and care.

Know Yourself and Work With Yourself

As I am writing this chapter, there are at least three potential clients that I need to follow up with and have not. One person gave a verbal "yes" on a discovery call, but she needed more time to fully step in to work together. The other was a "let's discuss later next month" and "revisit" over some direct messages. And one responded with questions to my weekly email about an upcoming writing community opportunity. I responded to all immediately or in the moment of the call/messages. However, I have offered no additional follow-up support. And I know why: because I am scared they will say "no" to working together.

See, one thing I have learned about myself as a person and business owner is that I still struggle with rejection. And while I know the idea that one person's "no" can lead to the next person's "yes," I often will avoid the inevitable and leave things hanging, so to speak. What I have also learned is that indecision does not feel good energetically for me. I would rather support someone with an aligned "no," than leave them dangling in no-response land. It took me a while to figure out how to navigate the discomfort of following up, even when I knew the client was likely not a good fit or likely not going to work with me. Yet learning to feel my way through that discomfort was far more *comfortable* than leaving people floating in indecision, including myself. Now, I do my best to set boundaries around people's decision-making process, even when doing so pushes me outside of my comfort zone. Here are some words I use to help me do that:

On a discovery call, I'll say something like: "Part of my intention for this call is to get to know you, and get to know if my team and I can help you. If I think we can, I'll tell you how we can work together, and I'll help you come to an aligned decision during our time together. How does that sound?"

When messaging back and forth has gone stale, I'll write something like: "Hey, did you still want help with ____?"

If someone needs more time to decide, I'll say something like: "I totally understand that you might feel you need more time, and I want to support you as you decide. Let's set up a follow-up call on ____, and here are some guiding questions to complete before coming to that call."

Then, I do my best to do what I say I will while also being honest when something is no longer doable or something needs to change. When I realize a client is not a good fit to work together right now, I will share that in a kind and loving way and refer them to other resources in the meantime.

Final Words

You don't have to *feel* like a professional to *act* like one.

If you're waiting until you feel 100% confident, credentialed, and polished to show up like a pro, you'll be waiting forever. The confidence you're craving comes from experience, and experience comes from doing the thing.

You are allowed to be growing and still be trustworthy.
You are allowed to be new and still be excellent.
You are allowed to use free tools and still deliver powerful results.

So, send the email. Take the payment. Offer the session. Mess up, fix it, and try again.

You don't need to hustle harder. You need to shift how you're showing up.

CHAPTER 9

The Business of Boundaries

HOW TO PROTECT YOUR ENERGY SO YOU
DON'T RESENT THE VERY THING YOU BUILT

The Ironic "Cost" of Freedom

There's something hilarious (and a little tragic) about leaving your 9–5 to be "free" … only to realize you've just created a 24/7 business where your boss is *you*—and she never stops working.

Early entrepreneurship can feel like a blurry soup of:

- ★ Clients texting you at 9:37pm
- ★ Saying yes to "just one more" thing
- ★ Doing 47 things that weren't even on your actual to-do list
- ★ Sitting down to write content and accidentally getting sucked into DMs, emails, and Canva purgatory

Boundaries aren't just a nice-to-have.
They're *infrastructure for sustainability*—especially when you're building something big, bold, and personal.

Without Boundaries, Burnout Is Inevitable

This part is so important, let's put it in bold:

When you build a business without boundaries, it will eventually become a job you resent.

This is how people "make it" and still feel miserable. It's how launches bring in money but drain your soul. It's how something you once *loved* feels like a burden you can't put down.

And the worst part? People will applaud you for it.
"You're so dedicated."
"You're always so responsive!"
"I don't know how you do it all."

Here's your permission to stop being available to everyone *at the cost of yourself.*

Why Boundaries Feel So Damn Hard

Especially for those of us who are ...

* Recovering people-pleasers
* Caretakers
* Empaths
* Trauma survivors
* Conditioned to believe our worth = being helpful and nice

... it can feel *terrifying* to say no, take up space, or disappoint someone.

I used to view boundaries as walls, as though I was sending someone or something away if I honored my values with boundaries. When in reality, they bring us closer because they bring clarity. They serve as containers. They're how we teach people how to work with us—not walk over us.

The Pressure to Respond

I use an app called Voxer to communicate with clients asynchronously. I love it. My business partner, Cindy, loves it, and our clients love it. The app allows us to text, send voice messages up to 15 minutes long, send images, and more. All of this allows me to feel connected to clients while not sharing my cell phone number and not clogging up my email. It is a deliverable that works for me.

Our clients know that we generally *work* Monday through Friday generally from 8am to 5pm, but that it may take up to 24 hours for us to respond to a new message. These basic boundaries of time work for me. However, incorporating communication tools, whatever they are, into any work with clients, can lend itself to feeling pressure to respond. Most of us can quickly see a notification and think ...

- ★ "Oh, they need me!"
- ★ "What if this is a potential client?"
- ★ "If I don't respond quickly, then ..." (insert all sorts of ridiculous stories we tell ourselves)

Recently, while enjoying a lovely, chill weekend with my teenager, I started to see my Voxer app blowing up more than usual. It is not uncommon for me to see a few messages come in over the weekend. But because of my clear boundaries around time, our clients know I am not going to respond until Monday at the earliest. Yet this time, when I saw message after message coming in, I started to panic. This particular client was close to publication, and I knew they had questions about the options in font, sizing, design, etc. we were considering for their cover.[5] I also knew the decisions around an author's cover can be a fun, exciting, as well

5. I am intentionally using "they/their" in the third-person singular to maintain anonymity of the client.

as potentially daunting moment in the publication process. So, naturally, I heavily considered opening up the messages and responding. Then, I remembered my boundaries. I remembered what was most important in that moment–the time with my family. I put the phone down and carried on with my day.

Come Monday, when both Cindy and I started reading and reviewing the messages from the client, I smiled and patted myself on the back for choosing to honor my boundaries. Because I left the client alone, they used the Voxer chat to make notes and talk themselves through all the decisions they were pondering, sprinkling in hilarious and sarcastic moments of frustration and revelations throughout. All decisions had been made without any response from me or my team. Had I chosen to interject, and bust through my response time boundary, the client would not have experienced the same resilience and clarity. Boundaries allowed both of us to receive exactly what we needed at that moment.

Now, let's talk about how we figure out what your boundaries actually are!

Try This: Build Your Boundary Blueprint

Let's get real. You don't need more vague advice about "self-care" and "protecting your peace." You need tangible, direct-as-hell business boundaries.

Start by asking yourself:

- ★ What are my non-negotiables for how I work?
- ★ What modes of communication feel supportive

versus draining?

- ★ What are my actual working hours?
- ★ How many clients or commitments can I realistically hold at once?

Then create boundaries around:

- ★ Time → Use calendar blocks, recurring CEO days, and scheduled rest.
- ★ Communication → Have clear email/DM response times and expectations.
- ★ Capacity → Know your yes. Know your no. Honor your capacity.
- ★ Money → Enforce payment deadlines. Stop giving discounts out of guilt.
- ★ Energy → Pay attention to the "invisible drains." These matter too.

You don't need to justify your boundaries. Sharing, "Here is how I work best" is enough.

Boundaries Are a Form of Self-Respect

You are *allowed* to …

- ★ Say, "I don't have the capacity for that right now"
- ★ Charge for your time, energy, and brilliance
- ★ Close your laptop when you're tired, not just when everything is "done"
- ★ Not be available 24/7—even if you work from home
- ★ Change your mind when something no longer aligns

You don't owe anyone access to your life just because they follow you or once bought something.

This is *your* business. You get to decide how it runs.

Try This Reframe

Next time you feel guilty for setting a boundary, say:

"I'm not being rude. I'm being rooted."

Rooted in your values.
Rooted in your capacity.
Rooted in your *actual vision,* not the one people are projecting onto you.

Boundaries aren't about pushing people away. They're about staying close to yourself.

Final Words

The longer you build your business, the more you'll realize this truth: sustainability is greater and more valuable than hustle.

The world doesn't need another burnt-out business owner. It needs *you*—fully expressed, deeply resourced, and able to do your work *without* falling apart.

Let your boundaries be a declaration: "I am not available for building my dream at the cost of my well-being."

You're not
doing it
wrong—
you're doing
it bravely.

Boundary-Setting Worksheet

BUILD A BUSINESS THAT SUPPORTS YOUR
LIFE—AND NOT THE OTHER WAY AROUND.

PART 1: Identify What's Important to You

Before you can set a boundary, you have to know what you're actually protecting. Answer these reflective prompts to uncover your core needs and values.

What do I need more of in my life and business (e.g., rest, creative space, quiet, clarity, freedom, income, support, flexibility)?

_____

_____

What activities, people, or patterns drain me the most right now (e.g., texting with clients after hours, last-minute requests, always being "on")?

_____

_____

_____

When do I feel most alive, empowered, or "in flow"? (Think about what environments, times of day, or types of work bring out your best.)

_____

_____

_____

What are my *non-negotiables*—the things I know
I need in place to function well (e.g., no calls after
5pm, one full day off per week, solo creative time
each morning)?

_____

_____

_____

PART 2: Define + Communicate Your Boundaries

Now that you've got clarity, let's make it practical. For
each of the categories below, jot down:

1. Your Desired Boundary
2. How You'll Communicate It
3. How You'll Adjust or Reinforce It Over Time

TIME
Where is your time going, and how do you want to
claim it back?

_____

_____

_____

- ★ **Boundary Example**: I only take meetings
  Tues–Thurs, 11am–3pm.
- ★ **Communication Plan**: Add it to my scheduler +

include it in onboarding emails.
- ★ **Alignment Check-In**: Review calendar monthly to see if it still works for me.

COMMUNICATION
When, where, and how do you want to be available?

_____

_____

_____

- ★ **Boundary Example**: I don't check DMs for client work. All business communications go through email.
- ★ **Communication Plan**: Set auto-responders + add to Instagram bio and client guide.
- ★ **Alignment Check-In**: Revisit inbox boundaries quarterly or after launches.

CAPACITY
How much can you realistically take on right now?

_____

_____

_____

- ★ **Boundary Example**: I take only 3 client projects per month.
- ★ **Communication Plan**: Add this limit to my services page + create a waitlist link.

- ★ **Alignment Check-In**: Ask myself monthly: Am I stretched too thin or in flow?

ENERGY + MONEY
Where does your energy go, and does your pricing reflect that?

_____

_____

_____

- ★ **Boundary Example**: No unpaid discovery calls; clients book a 30-min intro session for $____.
- ★ **Communication Plan**: Update my offer page and pricing policy.
- ★ **Alignment Check-In**: Re-evaluate rates and energy trade every 3–6 months.

Gentle Reminders

- ★ Boundaries are meant to evolve. You're not "failing" if they need to shift.
- ★ Not everyone will love your boundary—and that doesn't mean it's wrong.
- ★ Clarity is kind. The more direct you are, the smoother your client experience will be.

Repeat after me: My needs are valid. My time is valuable. My energy is sacred.

Now, go update that calendar, rewrite that FAQ page, or practice saying:

"Thanks for asking—here's how I'm handling that moving forward."

Other Things I Wish I Knew + No BS Tips to Building an Online Business with Intention

While the focus of this guidebook is to share the authentic, emotional journey of starting an online business, and sh*t I wish I had known earlier, I wanted to speak to a few common questions from my clients regarding more of the practical aspects of business creation. This is not an exhaustive list, and my responses come from my own experiences being a business owner for eight years (at this point), having multiple degrees and certifications, and having worked with many renowned business coaches and communities. I consider this the "quick and dirty" way to spend less time on some things that are important, yes, but not needed to get going on your dreams!

When do I need a website?

Spoiler: Not yet.

I was adamant that I *had* to have a website before I started working with my first online coaching client. Why? Because as a former teacher, I wanted to create videos and PDFs to give my clients support between sessions—like a little self-paced curriculum tucked into my site.

The reality? My first client didn't log in. Not even once. The client didn't use the portal, didn't access any of the PDFs, and didn't even read the cute little welcome message I wrote.

Turns out I could've just emailed the resources. Or dropped them into a free Google Drive folder (which, let's be honest, is what I do most often now anyway).

Here's the truth: you do **not** need a website. Or business cards. Or even a fancy business email address to work with people. You only need three things:

- ★ Something to offer
- ★ A way to get paid
- ★ Someone to work with

That's it. Sure, a website can eventually help showcase your work, share testimonials, and make you easier to find—but in the early days, it's often just a distraction disguised as productivity. It can eat up your time, your energy, and your money *before you've* validated your offer.

So, if you feel the urge to build a website, pause and ask:

> What's the story I'm telling myself
> about why I need this?

Is it truly about supporting your clients—or soothing your own fear of not looking "legit" enough? You can build something real before you ever build a website. I promise.

WTF is an LLC, and do I need one?

Spoiler: Probably—just not right this second.

Let's get one thing straight: I'm not a tax or financial expert. You should absolutely talk to an expert in your country or state before making any official business decisions.

Now that we've got that disclaimer out of the way …

LLC stands for **Limited Liability Company**, and it's a legal and tax classification that separates *you* (the person) from *your business* (the entity). It creates a layer of protection between your personal finances and your business dealings.[6]

When I first started my small massage therapy practice, I was a sole proprietor. I had a separate bank account to help keep things organized, but it was still under my personal name. About a year in, I registered as an LLC—mostly for the added protection and peace of mind.

Here's what it involved:

- ★ Filling out a few forms (varies by state in the U.S.)
- ★ Paying a one-time or annual fee
- ★ Naming my LLC (pro tip: don't stress too hard on the name—more on that in a sec)

---

6. "Limited Liability Company." Internal Revenue Services. Last Updates Feb. 15, 2025. https://www.irs.gov/businesses/small-businesses-self-employed/limited-liability-company-llc

Was it scary at first? A little.
Was it complicated? Not really.

There are tons of free resources online that walk you through how to set one up in your state, or you can use a service that does it for you (just be mindful of recurring charges and upsells).

Also, a common misconception: **your LLC name doesn't have to match your business name.** You can create DBAs ("doing business as" names) under your LLC if you operate under multiple identities or brands. For example, one of my LLCs is **Synergy Wellness Group LLC**, and under that umbrella I have **Synergy Publishing Group**—a separate DBA for a distinct part of my business.

Bottom line: you will probably want to form an LLC eventually, especially as your business grows. But you don't need to do it on day one. Get your offer out there, start working with people, and then circle back to this once you've got some momentum.

No need to make it more intimidating than it needs to be.

What about creating online courses? Yay or nay?

Spoiler: Do not start here. They are not as easy as they look.

I've got strong opinions about online courses. And they're not just coming from my experience as an online business owner—they're also shaped by two decades of teaching, including years spent designing and running online college courses.

Here's the bottom line: Online courses are *everywhere* in the online business world, and while they can be amazing, they are **not** the best place to start.

Why? Let me break it down:

* Well-designed courses take **a lot** of time and energy to build.
* Creating good content—videos, guides, PDFs— requires actual teaching skill and strategy. Not everyone has that background (and that's okay!).
* Most people build the entire course before ever selling it. That means weeks or months of unpaid labor … for something you don't even know will sell.
* Courses usually sell at a lower price point than coaching or group programs, meaning you need more buyers to make the same income. (Example: Would you rather sell **50 people a $100 course** or **2 people a $2,500 offer**?)
* To make real money from a course, you typically need a **large, warm audience** that's ready to buy.
* Launching a course well often requires systems,

strategy, and support—especially if you want to avoid burnout.

Now, let me say this with love:

Many people start with online courses because they're scared.

Scared of being seen. Scared to make offers. Scared they won't know what to say in a real-time client session.

So instead of addressing those fears, they build a course. It feels productive—"What? I'm still working on my course!"—but it often becomes a form of *business avoidance* dressed up as busywork.

Here's the truth most people won't say out loud: most courses don't create the transformation people are actually craving. Not because courses are bad, but because transformation usually requires real-time support, accountability, and connection. (You know, the stuff that happens when you *actually work with people.*)

Have I taken online courses to grow my business? Yes. Have I completed every single one of them? Absolutely not.
Have some of them been valuable? For sure, but not in the life-changing, this-built-my-business-from-the-ground-up kind of way.

If you're thinking about launching your business with a course, here's my invitation: **pause.**

Check in with yourself. Ask:

- ★ Is this the best next step for my business right now?
- ★ Or am I hiding behind a course because I'm afraid of offering my work directly?

Most successful course creators didn't start by building a course. They started by working with real people through one-on-one coaching, small groups, or workshops. They figured out what helped clients *actually* get results. *Then*, they turned those lessons into a course.

Even better? They pre-sold a "live" version of the course first—offering weekly calls or real-time content—so they could create it *as they went* based on the needs of their clients.

That's how you:

- ★ Get paid *while* creating your content
- ★ Build a course based on real transformation
- ★ Collect testimonials and proof that it works
- ★ Avoid getting stuck in perfectionism and isolation

So ... courses? Maybe, eventually. But start by working with real humans first. Your future course (and your future income) will thank you for it.

How can I create content when I am not a talented writer, content creator, digital marketer, etc.?

Spoiler: Be real, be you. Your people will love it!

If you've ever stared at a blinking cursor thinking, *"Who am I to share this?"*—welcome. You're not alone. In fact, this is one of the core reasons I wrote my book *Writing Is Not That Hard: Empowering the Writer Within.* I opened it with a quote by Irish poet Máirtín Ó Direáin:

> "My people spent most of their lives speaking poetry without realising it."

And after working with hundreds of writers and business owners over the years, I can confirm: you are likely *already speaking* poetry. You just don't see it yet.

Every single one of us bumps into fears when we try to share our voice online. Whether you're writing a newsletter, filming a reel, or hitting "publish" on your first blog post, the same doubts come up:

- ★ Am I making any sense?
- ★ Will anyone actually care?
- ★ Am I saying this the "right" way?

Here's the truth: **None of that matters as much as you think it does.** Your audience isn't looking for perfect grammar or polished transitions. They're looking for someone who feels *real*.

So instead of worrying about whether your content sounds "professional" or "correct," focus on creating from your heart. Share what you care about. Speak directly to the people you want to serve. Let them see who you are and why this work matters to you.

And if the idea of designing, formatting, or organizing content overwhelms you—good news: there are tools to help. Here are some of my everyday favorites:

- ★ **Canva**: Great for making content look beautiful. You can easily create on-brand posts, simple logos, and graphics for social media—even if you have zero design experience.
- ★ **Google Docs**: Basic, yes. But powerful. I draft all my emails, landing pages, and captions here. The built-in grammar checker and formatting tools are a lifesaver.
- ★ **AI Tools (like ChatGPT or Gemini)**: These can be helpful brainstorming buddies, especially if you're feeling stuck. But remember: your voice is the secret sauce. AI can support you, but it can't *replace* you.
- ★ **Instagram**: Still one of the easiest ways to share bite-sized, authentic content. Stories, reels, and posts can be downloaded and reused across platforms—and with a little music or text overlay, your message can really shine.

These tools are not fancy or new. But they've helped me show up consistently and authentically over the years, with no need to be a full-time content machine.

So if you're not a "writer" or a "marketer," guess what? That's not a problem. Start with your truth. Speak to your people. Let it be messy and human and *you*. You don't need to be a content expert—you just need to be yourself.

When can I quit my soul-sucking job?

Spoiler: It depends—but probably not as quickly as you'd like

I know, I know. You're ready to burn it all down and never sit through another awkward Zoom meeting or be micromanaged ever again. I get it. I really do.

I started my massage practice in 2017, followed by my online coaching business in 2018. But I didn't leave my full-time teaching job until the spring of 2021—**three full years** after starting my online business. And yes, waiting that long, nearly broke me. But looking back, I'm grateful I gave myself the time.

Here's why:

* ★ It usually takes around three years to build a business that can fully support you.
* ★ **Year 1:** Flails, fails, and figuring it out. You're experimenting, learning, making your first offers, and trying not to panic.
* ★ **Year 2:** You see traction—clients trickle in, offers improve, money begins to flow (unevenly, but it's happening).
* ★ **Year 3:** You've built some confidence, refined your systems, and you're generating more consistent income.
* ★ **Keeping your full-time job while you grow your business can actually help you succeed.** It gives you financial stability, access to health insurance, and a buffer for your nervous system. You'll make better, more aligned choices when

you're not operating from fear or scarcity.

★ **Even if you hate your job, it might still be a powerful launchpad.** I know it feels soul-sucking. But weirdly, having that "cushion" can give you the freedom to take bold action in your business—without putting pressure on it to perform instantly.

And still … no matter how strategic you are, **leaving your job will always require a leap of faith.** There's no magical moment where it stops being scary. People might not understand. You might doubt yourself. That's normal.

So when should you quit? Only you can answer that. But I'll leave you with this:

Don't rush the process just because you're tired.
Quit when your business can hold you.
Quit when you trust your capacity to figure things out.
Quit when your "yes" feels clear—not desperate.

And if it helps, your timeline doesn't have to look like anyone else's. What matters most is that it feels aligned, grounded, and true to *you*.

When should I invest in a coach/support?

Spoiler: Yesterday. Seriously.

One of the best decisions I've made as a business owner—and as a human—is investing in mentorship, coaching, and community support. I will *always* have a coach and/or a support system in my life. Not because I can't do things on my own, but because I *shouldn't* have to.

To date, I've invested well over $100,000 in coaching certifications, retreats, workshops, courses, books, and hiring mentors. That number might sound shocking— until I tell you that my business is now worth over *six times* that amount. And I don't say that to brag. I say it because I know, with full-body certainty, that my business would not be where it is today without those investments.

And no, this isn't about that tired cliché "you have to spend money to make money." It's about energy**.** The energy to say, I believe in myself enough to invest in my growth.

Every time I've paid for support, I've noticed a shift. I show up more fully. I stay more accountable. I prioritize my emotional, mental, and even physical wellbeing—not just for me, but for the clients I serve and the change I want to create. Truthfully, I wouldn't feel in integrity asking someone to pay thousands of dollars to work with me if I wasn't also investing in myself. How can I ask others to take a leap I'm unwilling to take?

Receiving (and yes, *paying for*) support keeps you going. It grounds you. It helps you draw from someone else's wisdom instead of reinventing every wheel. And most of the time? It speeds up your growth far more than doing it all alone.

So when should you invest in support? As soon as you can. Start small if needed—but *start*.

You're worth backing.

When should I hire people to help me?

Spoiler: Sooner than you think, but not for the reasons you think.

Let's talk about hiring—because no matter how scrappy, skilled, or stubborn you are (hi, hello, it's me), you cannot and should not do everything yourself.

When I started my online business, my first official hire (outside of coaches and mentors) was a virtual assistant (VA). And that support changed everything. But if I could go back in time, I'd actually do things a little differently—not because I didn't need a VA, but because I now understand there are *multiple* types of "hiring" that can help you build a sustainable business and stay out of burnout.

Let's break them down:

1. Hire in Your Personal Life First
Before you run off looking for a fancy social media manager, ask yourself: What do I do every day that drains my energy and steals time from my business (and life)?

Laundry. Grocery shopping. Cleaning. Cooking. School drop-off. The constant tasks of running a household. These things take time—*a lot* of time. And often, hiring help here is cheaper than hiring business support. A meal prep service, house cleaner, or even Instacart can buy you back hours every week that you can pour into your business. If I were starting over, I would have hired in this category *first*.

2. Hire Outside Your Zone of Excellence

Early in my journey, I read *The Big Leap* by Gay Hendricks (highly recommend). He talks about how most of us spend our time in our *Zone of Excellence*—things we're good at but that don't light us up. Sound familiar?

I was coaching (my Zone of Genius), but also spending way too much time setting up email automations, designing graphics, and fiddling with backend tech (Zone of Excellence ... bordering on *Zone of Kill Me Now*).

This is where hiring a virtual assistant or someone for one-off projects can save your brain, your energy, and your soul.

3. Hire for What You Have Zero Desire to Learn

Eventually, you'll want to do something new—like redesign your website or finally deal with your taxes (ugh). There's no need to suffer through things that are *entirely outside your skillset* and *completely optional* for you to learn.

Hire someone whose *Zone of Genius* is your personal nightmare. There are people out there who *love* bookkeeping. People who love words and know all about publishing (hi, it's me again!). Let them live their best lives while you stay in yours.

There's no one-size-fits-all hiring roadmap, but I hope this helps you think about support in a more expansive way. Look at your current workload:

- ★ What drains you?
- ★ What energizes you?
- ★ What could someone else do faster, better, and with more joy?

You don't have to hire a full team right away. When I hired my VA, I didn't even know what I truly needed her to do. We started with five hours a week at $20/hour, which was strictly based on what I felt comfortable with. Her role has grown with my business, and so has my investment in her brilliance.

Start where you are. Start small if needed. But *start*. You don't have to do this alone … yep, I'm going to keep saying this!

What about the 3,357 other questions I have?!

Spoiler: You're not supposed to do this alone. (Told ya I'd keep saying this!)

First: SAME. I had 3,357 questions too (and probably still do). Starting an online business will crack you open, push every button, and leave you Googling things like "WTF is an email funnel" at 2am while eating peanut butter off a spoon. There's no magical checklist that answers everything. And honestly? That's part of what makes this path so powerful.

You're not supposed to know it all. You're not supposed to do it all by yourself. You *are* supposed to follow the tug. You *are* allowed to get support. And that's exactly where I come in.

If you've read this far and felt something stir—whether it was clarity, inspiration, a sense of *finally* feeling like someone gets you, or even just a sigh of relief—I want to invite you into deeper support. I work with amazing, mission-driven humans who are starting and growing their heart-centered, values-aligned, online businesses, especially those who feel like the traditional ways of doing business don't quite fit who they are or how they move in the world.

I help people like you turn their lived experience, skills, and gifts into offers that heal, empower, and *actually sell*. I do it through a mix of coaching, strategy, and loving ass-kicking. I believe you don't have to hustle to succeed—but you *have* to be brave, get clear, and surround yourself with the right people.

If you want that kind of support, I'd love to connect.

Because you are reading this book, you can schedule a chat with me to get clear on your next best steps! **Book your session at synergypublishinggroup.com/schedule.**

Whether it's a private coaching container, a writing retreat, or a group program, you'll be met with genuine support, real strategy, and a lot of heart. Because your business doesn't just change *your* life. It ripples outward. It creates impact. It matters.

You matter. Now go get after it—and if you need a guide along the way, you know where to find me.

About the Author

Shana V. Hartman, PhD, is a former university English professor turned embodied writing coach. She built a business based on her values of freedom and empowerment. She helps heart-centered professionals and thought leaders share the core messages from their life and career experiences in powerful books by using an embodied writing approach that allows people to truly experience their transformative words. Her clients build amazing businesses and legacies from those books. She is a published author many times over, Founding Partner of Synergy Publishing Group, and Managing Partner of Synergy House LLC. As an ICF certified coach and BodyMind Method© Coach, Shana supports her people in connecting with their inner truth, writing from that place, and creating a life that makes an impact. She truly believes in the power of leaving a legacy with your words. When she's not writing or helping others with their writing, Shana enjoys ballroom dancing, traveling, and spending time with her amazing theater kid and checking if her grown stepdaughters (finally) texted her back.

Learn more about Shana and her work
by connecting with her on Instagram
@theshana_v
@synergypublishinggroup

You can schedule a chat with Shana to get clear on your next best steps! **Book your session at synergypublishinggroup.com/schedule.**